CAMBRIDGE
UNIVERSITY PRESS

CAMBRIDGE
Global English Starters

Learner's Book B

Kathryn Harper & Gabrielle Pritchard

Welcome!

Cambridge Global English is a ten-stage course for learners of English as a Second Language (ESL). The ten stages range from the beginning of primary (Starters–Stage 6) to the end of lower secondary (Stages 7–9). It is ideal for all international ESL learners, and particularly for those following the Cambridge Primary and Lower Secondary English as a Second Language Curriculum Frameworks, as it has been written to adhere to these frameworks.

In addition to Learner's Book B, *Cambridge Global English Starters Activity Book B* provides supplementary support and practice. *Cambridge Global English Starters Fun with Letters and Sounds B* offers intensive practice in reading and writing the upper- and lower-case letters learnt in lesson 4a of each unit. Comprehensive support for teachers is available in the *Cambridge Global English Starters Teacher's Resource*.

The following icons are used in this Learner's Book:

- Audio track number reference
- Differentiation
- Personalisation
- Critical thinking

For further explanation please refer to the teacher's resource.

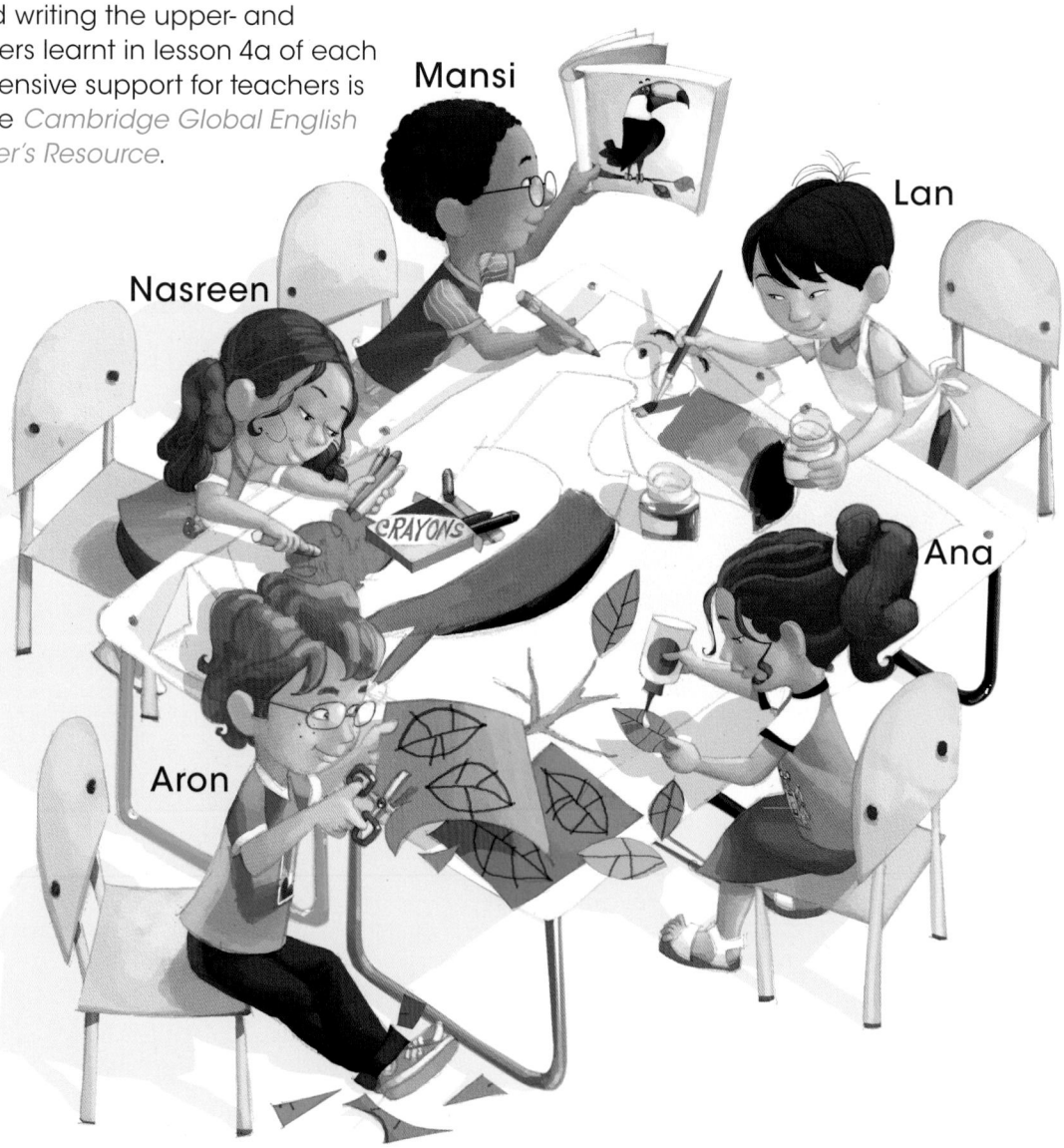

Contents

4 Play time!

Lesson 1	Introduction to unit theme: Play time! Words: ***ball, balloon, bike, game, kite, puzzle***	4
Lesson 2	Story time: *Our fun day* Words: ***purple, pink, bounce, fly, scared, ride, play*** Values: How can we help others?	6
Lesson 3	Focus: Play and make Language and words: ***Can you (make)? Yes, I can.*** ***play, make, teddy bear, music, cake, climb a tree, tap knees, jump, bee, sing*** Song: *Can you climb a tree?*	10
Lesson 4a	Letters and sounds: ***j, k, l***	12
Lesson 4b	Numbers: ***5, 6***	13
Lesson 5	CLIL: PE – fun exercises	14
Lesson 6	Project: Make a game	16

5 Let's eat!

Lesson 1	Introduction to unit theme: Food Words: ***apples, carrots, mangoes, onions, peppers, spinach***	18
Lesson 2	Story time: *The greedy goat* Words: ***orange, brown, greedy, angry, goat, rabbit, duck*** Values: Why is it bad to be greedy?	20
Lesson 3	Focus: What do you like? Language & words: ***I (like/don't like), He/She (likes/doesn't like),*** ***They (like/don't like), potatoes, nuts, lettuce, rubbish bin*** Song: *That greedy goat*	24
Lesson 4a	Letters and sounds: ***m, n, o***	26
Lesson 4b	Numbers: ***7, 8***	27
Lesson 5	CLIL: Science – sweet and salty foods	28
Lesson 6	Project: Make a poster puzzle	30

6 Let's listen!

Lesson 1	Introduction to unit theme: Music Words: ***fast, high, loud, low, quiet, slow***	32
Lesson 2	Story time: *The tiger and the woodpecker* Words: ***tiger, woodpecker*** Values: Why do we say 'sorry'?	34
Lesson 3	Focus: What can you hear? Language and words: ***What can you hear? I can hear, drum,*** ***guitar, piano, flute, wind, bird*** Song: *What can you hear?*	38
Lesson 4a	Letters and sounds: ***p, q, r***	40
Lesson 4b	Numbers: ***1–8***	41
Lesson 5	CLIL: Interpreting sounds, associating sounds with emotions	42
Lesson 6	Project: Make an instrument	44

Review Units 4–6 46

Please see the teacher's resource for complete scope and sequence.

4 Play time!

1 Think about it How do we have fun?

1 Chant and clap.

A puzzle or game,
A balloon or ball,
A bike or kite,
There's fun for all.

2 What can you see?
Explore the picture.

Unit 4 Lesson 1 Words: ball, balloon, bike, game, kite, puzzle **Listen/Say:** chant, sticking activity, game

3 Listen, say and stick.

ball
kite
bike
balloon
game
puzzle

4 Play the game.

Can you remember the toys?
Pass the ball. Choose and say.

2 Story time

Our fun day

3 **1 Listen and follow the story.**

Look at the pictures. What are they playing with?

Unit 4 Lesson 2 Words: purple/pink, bounce, fly, scared, ride, play **Listen/Read:** story **Speaking:** acting out story, talking about games, helping others

5
Let's try the bikes.
Can you ride a bike, Jake?
Yes!
6
This bike is very big. I'm scared !
7
You can ride the bike now.
Thank you.
8
?
Look! Can you find the pink ball ?

Unit 4 Lesson 2 Words: purple/pink, bounce, fly, scared, ride, play **Listen/Read:** story **Speaking:** acting out story, talking about games, helping others

2a What can they do?

Look at the story and match.

Rami can

Jake can

Amaya can

Jake can't

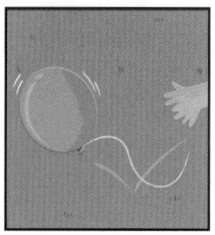

2b Who can play the game?

Tick ✓.

☐

☐

☐

3 What can you do with a ball and a balloon?

Talk.

4 Act out the story.

5 Values

How can we help others?

3 Talk about it Playing – making and doing

1a Look at what we do for fun.

What do we play with? What do we make?

1b Draw lines to match to the correct box.

play

make

1c Ask and answer.

2 Play the colour game.

Give clues and guess.

Unit 4 Lesson 3 Words: play/make, teddy bear, music, cake, climb a tree, tap knees, jump, bee, sing **Language:** Can you (make music)? Yes, I can. **Listen/say:** game, song

3a Look and tick ✓ the things **you** can do.

3b Listen, sing and act out.

Song: Can you climb a tree?

Can you play with me?
Can you climb a tree?
Yes, I can.
I can climb a tree.

Can you play with me?
Can you count to 3?
Yes, I can.
I can climb a tree.
I can count to 3.

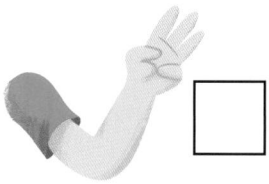

Can you play with me?
Can you tap your knees?
Yes, I can.
I can climb a tree.
I can count to 3.
I can tap my knees.

Can you play with me?
Can you jump quickly?
Yes, I can.
I can climb a tree.
I can count to 3.
I can tap my knees.
I can jump quickly.

Can you play with me?
Can you buzz like a bee?
Yes, I can.
I can climb a tree.
I can count to 3.
I can tap my knees.
I can jump quickly.
I can buzz like a bee.

Can you play with me?
Can you sing loudly?
Yes, I can.
I can climb a tree.
I can count to 3.
I can tap my knees.
I can jump quickly.
I can buzz like a bee.
I can sing loudly!

4a Let's learn our ABC

5 **1a** Listen, point and say.

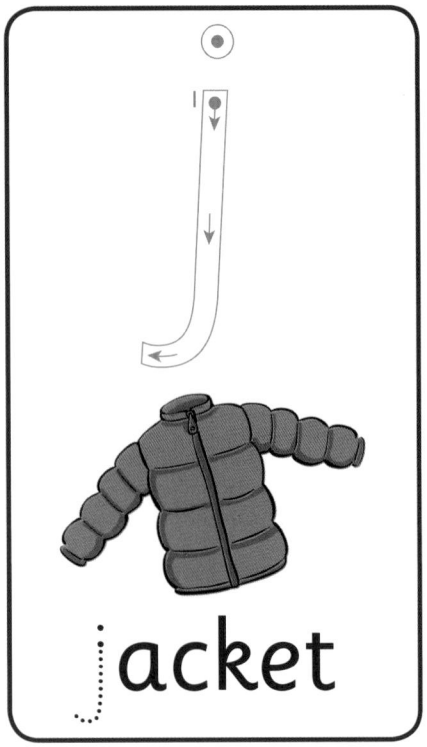

6 **1b** Listen, find and trace.

7 **2a** Listen and say.

2b Which pictures are missing?

Listen again. Then join and colour.

Unit 4 Lesson 4a Letters/sounds: j, k, l **Words:** jacket, kite, leaf **Lesson 4b Numbers:** 5, 6 **Listen/speak:** song **Write:** numbers 1–6

4b Let's learn our numbers

1 Look and say.

Write the numbers.

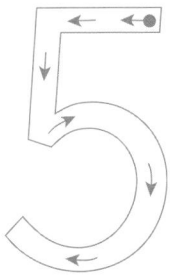

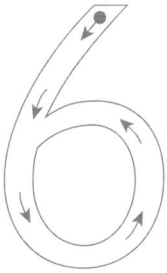

8 2a Listen and sing.

1, 2, 3,
I can see
3 big balloons
Flying up to the moon.

1, 2, 3,
4, 5, 6,
I can see
6 big balloons
Flying up to the moon.

Oh, no, no!
Now I can see
1 little bee
Flying up to the moon.

6, 5, 4,
3, 2, 1.
Oh, no, no!
The balloons are all gone.

2b Count and write.

5 Find out more Fun exercises

1a Can <u>you</u> do these things?

1b Stick the **yes** ☺ or **no** ☹ stickers.

Unit 4 Lesson 5 Words: kick, hop, jump **Listen/say:** doing actions, activities they like

2a Listen and do.

2b Which activities do you like?

Reflection

What makes an activity fun?

6 Our project

1a Make a game.

Work with friends. Think of a game that uses a ball or a balloon.

Try out your ideas.

1b Show your game to the class.

2 Play the games.

Take turns to play the games.

3 Tell the class.

Look what I can do!

I can:

- talk about how we have fun
- understand a story
- do PE activities
- identify and say the letters and sounds **j**, **k**, **l**
- count to 6

5 Let's eat!

1 Think about it What do we eat?

10 1 Chant and clap.

Spinach and carrots,
Peppers and onions,
Apples and mangoes,
What shall I grow?
I really don't know!

2 What can you see?
Explore the picture.

Unit 5 Lesson 1 Words: apples, carrots, mangoes, onions, peppers, spinach **Listen/Say:** chant, sticker activity, game

3 Listen and stick.

Listen, say and act.

4 Go shopping.

Play the game.

2 Story time

The greedy goat

12 **1 Listen and follow the story.**

Find the foods in the story.

1

I'm hungry.

I'm hungry.

I'm hungry.

2

Look **hot peppers**!
I don't like **peppers**.

I don't like **peppers**.

I like **peppers**.

3

1, 2, 3, 4, 5
hot peppers!

Yikes!

4

Look! Onions!
I don't like onions.

I don't like onions.

I like onions.

Unit 5 Lesson 2 Words: orange/brown, greedy, angry, goat, rabbit, duck **Listen/Read:** story **Speaking:** acting out story, food colours, food likes/dislikes, being greedy

5
1, 2, 3, 4, 5, 6 onions !
Boo hoo hoo!
6
Look! Spinach !
I like ☺spinach .
I like ☺spinach .
I like ☺spinach .
7
Yummy!
8
We are very angry!
I'm sorry.
You are a very greedy goat !

Unit 5 Lesson 2 Words: orange/brown, greedy, angry, goat, rabbit, duck **Listen/Read:** story **Speaking:** acting out story, food colours, food likes/dislikes, being greedy

2a What do Goat, Rabbit and Duck like?

2b What are the food colours?

Look and match. Then colour.

2c Some foods come in different colours.

Which ones are these?

3 Act out the story.

4 Values

Why is it bad to be greedy?

3 Talk about it What do you like?

1a Complete the maze and talk about what **you** like and don't like.

I like apples. I don't like peppers.

1b Look at your partner's maze and tell the class about it.

Khalid likes potatoes.

1c Do a group survey about the mazes.

Unit 5 Lesson 3 Words: potatoes, nuts, lettuce, rubbish bin **Language:** I (like/don't like) potatoes. He/She (likes/doesn't like) potatoes. They (like/don't like) potatoes.
Listen/say: game, song

Stickers for Unit 4 page 5

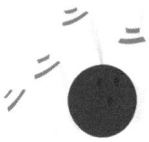

Stickers for Unit 4 page 14

Stickers for Unit 5 page 19

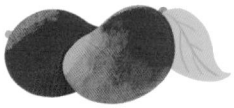

Stickers for Unit 5 page 28

Stickers for Unit 6 page 33

Stickers for Unit 6 page 42

2a Listen and clap when you hear a food word.

13 **2b** Listen, sing and act out.

Song: That greedy goat

Chorus:

Munch, munch, munch, munch,
Greedy goat's mouth's too full to sing.
Greedy goat likes everything!
Munch, munch, munch, munch.

That greedy, greedy, greedy goat,

Opens up his greedy throat,

Carrots, onions, apples in,

He is just a rubbish bin.

Greedy, greedy, greedy goat!

That greedy, greedy, greedy goat,

Opens up his greedy throat,

Mangoes, spinach, peppers in,

He is just a rubbish bin.

Greedy, greedy, greedy goat!

4a Let's learn our ABC

14 **1a Listen, point and say.**

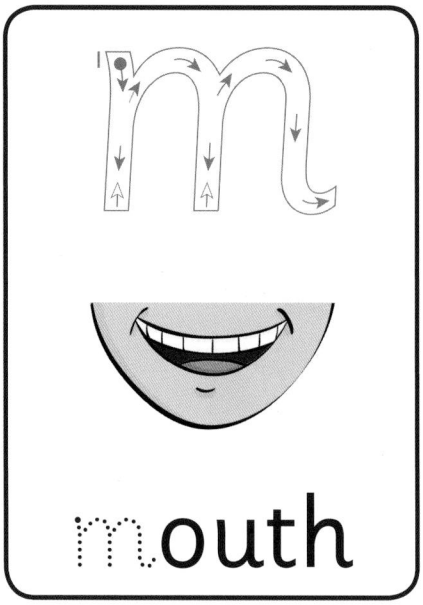

15 **1b Listen, find and trace.**

16 **2a Look at the picture.**

Then listen, find and repeat.

16 **2b Listen again.**

Trace the letters. Then circle the words.

mangonoseoctopusmouse

4b Let's learn our numbers

1 Look and say.

Write the numbers.

17

2a Listen and sing.

1, 2 grow on a tree.

Out comes the .

Now there are 1, 2, 3, 4 .

1, 2, 3, 4 grow on a tree.

Out comes the .

Now there are 1, 2, 3, 4, 5, 6 .

1, 2, 3, 4, 5, 6 grow on a tree.

Out comes the .

Now there are 1, 2, 3, 4, 5, 6, 7, 8 .

8 mangoes for you and me!

2b Count and write.

5 Find out more Sweet or savoury?

1a Are these things sweet or savoury?

What do you think?

18 1b Listen and stick.

Unit 5 Lesson 5 Words: sweet, savoury, rice, bananas, ice cream, crisps **Listen/say:** discussing foods, trying foods, talking about foods they like

2a Make a food experiment with real or pretend foods.

2b Ask your friends to try your foods.

2c Make a food poster.

Reflection

What kind of tastes do you like?
Savoury? Sweet? Spicy? Fruity?

6 Our project

1 Make a poster puzzle.

Work with friends.

Choose an animal. Find out what it likes to eat.

2 Make your poster puzzle with friends.

Make animal and food pictures. Stick the pictures on your poster puzzle.

3 Can your friends solve the poster puzzle?

Look what I can do!

I can:

- talk about food
- follow and understand a story about a greedy goat
- talk about foods I like and don't like
- identify and say the letters and sounds **m**, **n**, **o**
- count to 8
- talk about sweet and savoury food

6 Let's listen!

1 Think about it What can we hear?

19 **1 Chant and clap.**

Clap quietly, clap loudly,
Tap fast, tap slowly,
Sing high, sing low,
Now, let's go, go, go!

2 What can you see?
Explore the picture.

Unit 6 Lesson 1 Words: fast, high, loud, low, quiet, slow **Listen/Say:** chant, sticker activity, game

20

3 Listen, answer and stick.

Listen and clap.

4 Play the music game.

Choose a leader. Take turns to conduct the class.

2 Story time

The tiger and the woodpecker

21 **1 Listen and follow the story.**

What kind of noise does the bird make? Read, listen and find out.

1

I can run fast.

2

I can make a loud roar and jump.

3

Tap, tap, tap, tap, tap!

4

Quiet! Stop that tapping!

Unit 6 Lesson 2 Words: tiger, woodpecker **Listen/Read:** story, sounds **Speaking:** acting out story, saying story **Write:** trace words

5
Quiet!
No Tapping!
Sorry, Tiger. I can stop.
6
Now I can run and jump!
OUCH! I've got a stick in my mouth.
7
Please help me. I can't close my mouth. I can't eat.
8
Sorry. No tapping.
No Tapping!

Unit 6 Lesson 2 Words: tiger, woodpecker, sorry **Listen/Read:** story, sounds **Speaking:** acting out story, saying story **Write:** trace words

2 Trace what Tiger can do.

run

jump

roar

eat

fly

swim

3 What does Tiger <u>not</u> like? Tick ✓.

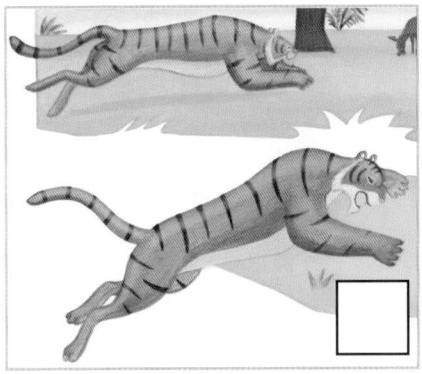
running and jumping

noisy birds

sticks in his mouth

rabbits

tapping

4 Look at frame 9. Why does Tiger change his mind?

21

5a Close your eyes and listen to the story.

Raise your hands high when it's noisy.
Put them down when it's quiet.

5b Make masks and act out the story.

6 Values
Why do we say 'sorry'?

3 Talk about it What can you hear?

1 Match the things to what you can and can't hear.

I can hear goats.

teddy bear

goat

can hear

drum

carrot

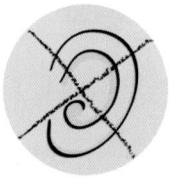

can't hear

bird

guitar

wind

tiger

sun

22 **2a Listen and say what you can hear.**
Write the numbers.

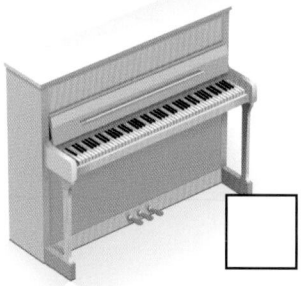

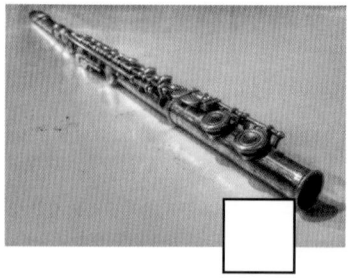

23 **2b Is it loud or quiet?**

24 **2c Is it fast or slow?**

I can hear a drum. It's fast.

Unit 6 Lesson 3 Words: drum, guitar, piano, flute, wind, bird **Language:** What can you hear? I can hear (a drum). It's (fast) **Listen/say:** game, song

25 **3a** Listen and match.

25 **3b** Listen, sing and act out.

Song: What can you hear?

Chorus:
Wiggle your ears.
What can you hear?
Wiggle your ears.
What can you hear?

Can you hear the drum?
Fast and slow.
Can you hear the flute?
High and then low.

Can you hear the guitar?
Fast and slow.
Can you hear the piano?
High and then low.

Now it's your turn.
What did you learn?
Can you sing
Just one little thing?

Go on ... sing!

4a Let's learn our ABC

26 **1a** Listen, point and say.

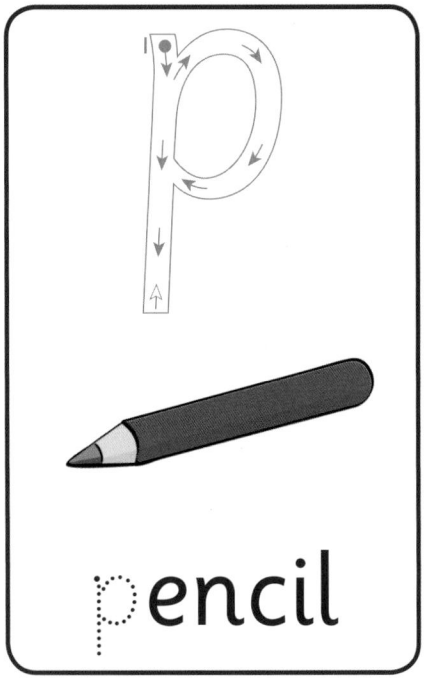

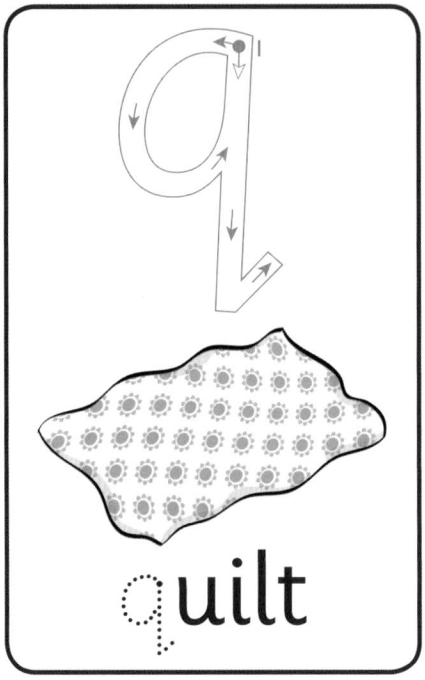

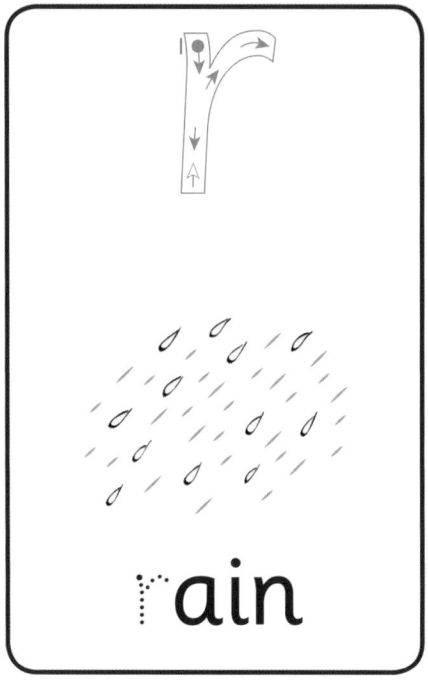

27 **1b** Listen, find and trace.

2a Join and write the letter.

28 **2b** Can you find the sounds in the picture?

Listen and write the letter.

_acket _ite _eaf _outh _ine _ctopus

Unit 6 Lesson 4a Letters/sounds: p, q, r **Words:** pencil, quilt, rain **Lesson 4b Numbers:** 1–8 **Listen/speak:** song **Write:** numbers 1–8

4b Let's learn our numbers

1 Look and say.

Write the numbers.

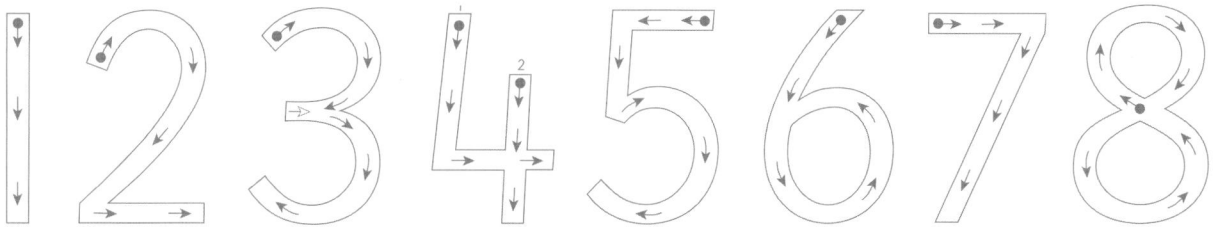

29

2a Listen and sing.

1, 2, 3, 4.
4 big bubbles float up high,
4 big bubbles float on by.

5, 6, 7, 8.
8 big bubbles float up high,
8 big bubbles float on by.

8, 7, 6, 5.
5 big bubbles float up high,
5 big bubbles float on by.

4, 3, 2, 1.
1 big bubble floats up high,
1 big bubble floats on by.

2b Count and write.

5 Find out more How does music make us feel?

1a Look and say the feeling words.

Add stickers for the new words.

happy ☐

sad ☐

excited ☐

scared ☐

relaxed ☐

like dancing ☐

30 1b Listen and describe each piece of music.

Is it fast or slow? Is it loud or quiet? Can you hear any instruments?

30 1c How do the songs make you feel?

Listen again and write numbers.

30 1d Listen again.

Which songs are easy to clap to?
Why? Which song do you like best?

Unit 6 Lesson 5 Words: relaxed, excited, dancing **Listen/say:** discussing emotions and music, describing music

2a Listen.

Make movements to go with the music.

2b Perform for the class.

3 Think of a song that makes you happy.

Sing it.

Reflection

When the music is fast, I feel …

When the music is slow, I feel …

6 Our project

1 Make an instrument.

Choose a drum or a shaker.

2a How to make a drum.

You need: a , a small, coloured , an elastic and .

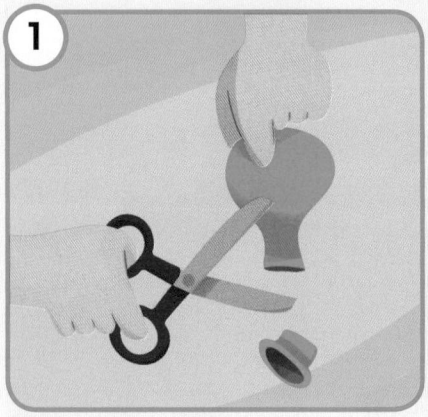

Cut.

Pull the over the . Put the elastic over the .

Stick .

2b How to make a shaker.

You need: a , a , different , and .

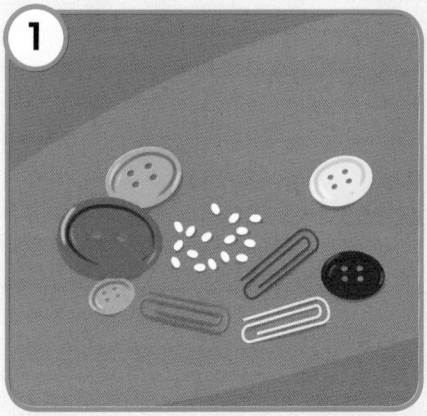

Choose and put in the .

Cut the and .

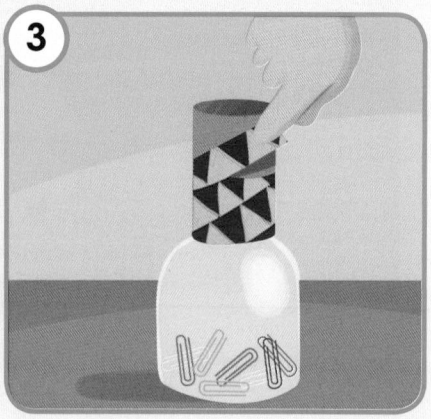

Stick .

3a Experiment with your instruments.

3b Make music.

Look what I can do!

I can:

- understand what we can and can't hear
- follow and understand a story about a tiger and a woodpecker
- talk about things I can hear
- identify and say the letters and sounds **p**, **q**, **r**
- use the numbers 1 to 8

What can we remember?

32 **1** Listen and draw lines.

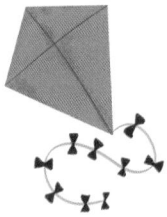

33

2 Count and write the numbers.

Then listen and check.

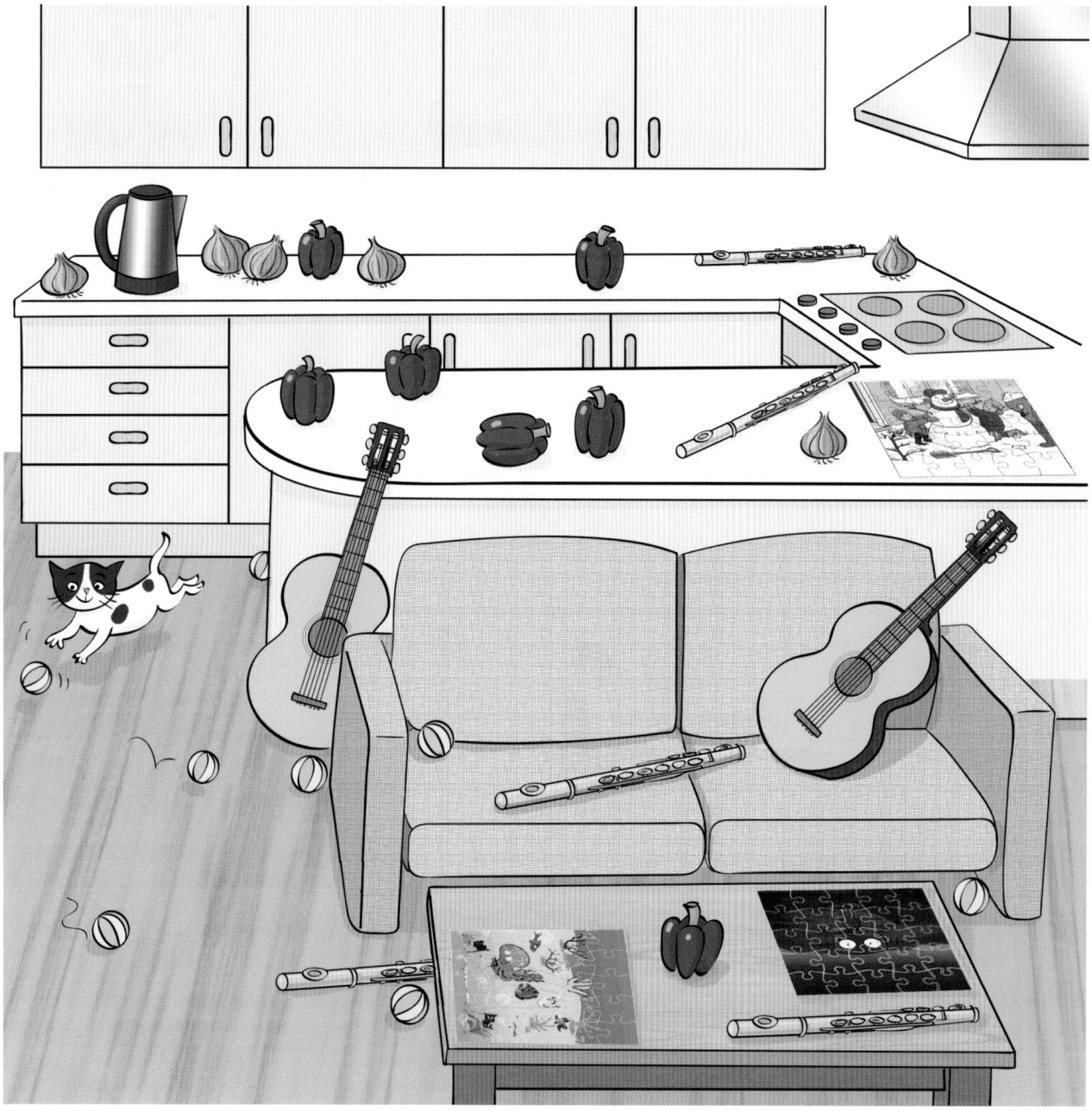

☐ flutes 

☐ guitars 

☐ onions 

☐ puzzles 

☐ peppers 

☐ balls 

34 3 Listen and tick ✓ the box.

1

a ☐

b ☐

c ☐

2

a ☐

b ☐

c ☐

3

a ☐

b ☐

c ☐

4

a ☐

b ☐

c ☐

5

a ☐

b ☐

c ☐